ATLANTIC

OCEAN

1 Compostela, where Coronado's expedition began in February, 1540.

2 Cíbola, a pueblo village where the Spaniards fought hostile Indians and Coronado was hit by a large rock.

3 Tule Canyon, where Coronado's men decided to let Sopete, rather than the Turk, lead them to Quivira.

4 Quivira, where the army was greeted by friendly Indians and the Turk was killed as a traitor.

5 Tiguex, the Spaniards' winter quarters, where Coronado fell from his horse.

 THE ASTROLABE, an instrument developed by the Greeks, is the symbol for World Explorer Books. At the time of Columbus, sailors used the astrolabe to chart a ship's course. The arm across the circle could be moved to line up with the sun or a star. Using the number indicated by the pointer, a sailor could tell his approximate location on the sea. Although the astrolabe was not completely accurate, it helped many early explorers in their efforts to conquer the unknown.

World Explorer Books are written especially for children who love adventure and exploration into the unknown. Designed for young readers, each book has been tested by the Dale-Chall readability formula. Leo Fay, Ph.D., Professor of Education at Indiana University, is educational consultant for the series. Dr. Fay, an experienced teacher and lecturer, is well known for his professional bulletins and text material in both elementary reading and social studies.

A WORLD EXPLORER

Francisco Coronado

BY FAITH YINGLING KNOOP

ILLUSTRATED BY DOM LUPO

GARRARD PUBLISHING COMPANY
CHAMPAIGN, ILLINOIS

To Kevin
who was born in Coronado, California

This series is edited by Elizabeth Minot Graves

Contents

1

Younger Son

Francisco had hardly tasted his favorite lunch of chicken and olives. He was listening to Father tell about the New World.

"Today a king's messenger brought news to Salamanca," his father, Juan Vásquez de Coronado, was saying. "Hernando Cortés is exploring new lands across the Ocean Sea."

Ten-year-old Francisco looked excitedly at Gonzalo, his older brother. Two little sisters sat beside the boys. Father was at one end of the table, Mother Isabel at the other. It was 1520, in Salamanca, Spain.

"Is Cortés finding gold?" Francisco asked his father.

Father nodded. "Yes, the Indians there have a lot of gold. Cortés is sending some back to Spain."

"You've met Cortés, haven't you, Father?" Gonzalo asked.

"Yes," Father said. "Cortés studied law at the great University here. He gave up law to explore the New World."

"I want to explore, too," Francisco said. "Don't you, Gonzalo?"

Gonzalo grinned back. "Of course." Then he teased his little sisters, "Don't you wish girls could be explorers?"

The little girls smiled, too young to understand.

It was now twenty-eight years since Columbus had crossed the Ocean Sea, or Atlantic Ocean. Columbus had discovered islands that he thought were part of Asia. Later explorers found them to be near two new continents, North and South America. Cortés was exploring today's Mexico. He was conquering the Aztec Indians there.

"I hope Cortés is converting the Indians to the Christian faith," Mother said softly.

"I hope so, too," Father said. He pushed back his chair. "Now, I have something else to tell you. This morning I signed my will. When I die, my house and land will go to Gonzalo, for he is the older son."

Francisco's blue eyes were puzzled. He

looked around the big dining room. Silver
plates gleamed on the table. Paintings and
gay hangings brightened the dark walls.
Outside was a courtyard with fragrant
flowers. The tinkle of the court's fountain
made pleasant music. "None of this will
belong to me?" Francisco asked.

"I am Lord of Coquilla," Father answered slowly. "There can be only one Lord of Coquilla. At my death, the title goes to Gonzalo. And with the title go my house and land."

Francisco sighed. "Then I won't live in our palace," he said.

The father smiled. "I am sure Gonzalo will invite you to visit him," he said. "This is only a small palace. In fact, we are not very rich. You younger children will be given enough money to get a start in life. But Gonzalo will need most of my money to keep up the palace. You will have to earn your living, Francisco. You must choose a career."

"Younger sons often study law," Mother Isabel said. "Or you might become a priest, Francisco."

Francisco shook his head. "I shall be

a soldier," he declared, "and go to the New World to live."

Gonzalo frowned. "You are the lucky one," he told his brother. "You will have adventure across the Ocean Sea. I must stay here whether I want to or not."

Francisco had another question. "Will I still be a nobleman?" he asked.

Juan Vásquez de Coronado smiled at his younger son. "Of course," he answered. "You will always be Francisco Vásquez de Coronado, a nobleman of Spain. Remember to do right, to be brave, and to be loyal to the King of Spain."

"And to serve God," added Mother Isabel.

"I'll remember," Francisco promised.

2

Off to Granada

The Coronado family was gathered in the courtyard to say good-bye to Francisco. Francisco, now in his late teens, was as tall as his father. His blue eyes sparkled. He was leaving home for knight's training at the King's court in Granada.

Francisco's sisters cried as they said good-bye. They were attending a convent school where they would become nuns.

There were two little brothers, now, Juan and Pedro. They cried, too, as Francisco lifted them up for good-bye hugs.

Gonzalo was a student at the University of Salamanca. He shook hands sadly. "I wish I were going with you," he told Francisco.

Just then a young man dashed into the courtyard. Iago was a friend of Gonzalo's. He taught mathematics at the University. "Good luck, Francisco," he cried. Suddenly his voice became dreamlike. "You will win a high place and much power in a distant land. . . . But beware of a bad fall which you may never get over." With these strange words, Iago was off.

The Coronados stood silent with surprise. Then Gonzalo spoke. "Don't let Iago worry you. He likes to tell fortunes. But they're not always right. Forget what he said."

But Francisco would never forget the words. It was his great hope to win power in the New World. Should he always be careful of falls?

Francisco and his father set out for Granada on horseback. Francisco was happy as they rode over the plains and mountains. At Granada he would learn to fight. In time he would become a knight, an officer in the army of King Charles of Spain.

After many days, the Coronados neared Granada. They pulled up their horses to look at the shining city ahead. "How beautiful it is!" gasped Francisco.

"That is the Alhambra on the hill above Granada," Father said, pointing it out. "It is really a little city in itself. Inside its walls are the royal castle and the government buildings. It was built by the

14

African Moors when they lived in Spain."

Francisco looked at the red stone castle. "My new home!" he whispered.

At the Alhambra, Father found his old friend, Antonio de Mendoza. Mendoza was head of the King's household. He had a black beard and dark eyes. He eyed Francisco sternly. "Your knight's training will start at once," he said.

Francisco bowed. He remembered his father's words, "Mendoza is strict but fair."

"Go with God," was Father Juan's good-bye.

3

A Spanish Knight

Francisco found life exciting in the knights' quarters in the Alhambra. Each night he fell onto his cot, tired but happy. Each morning he awoke eager for his lessons in riding and fighting.

Francisco learned to wheel his horse away from sudden enemy attacks. He learned to fight with dagger and sword. He learned, too, to be polite to everyone. He made many friends.

Often the Spanish knights held tournaments, or games of war, on the plain beside Granada. At first, Francisco helped the knights put on their heavy armor. He put armor on their horses too. Then he handed the knights their blunted lances, as they rode to the mock battle. Onlookers cheered for their favorites.

Finally, Francisco himself fought in a tournament. He and another horseman, armed with lances, tried to push each other off their horses. Francisco won, two out of three times.

His father's friend, Mendoza, was watching. Mendoza called Francisco to him. "You are a good fighter, Francisco," he said. "You will soon be ready for His Majesty's wars."

Francisco bowed. "I am ready to serve His Majesty in Europe if that is his wish.

But I have always hoped to go to New Spain. Cortés. . . ."

Mendoza's dark eyes flashed. "Cortés," he said, "has given great riches to Spain. But the King is not pleased with him. Cortés has been cruel to the Indians."

"I would carry out the King's wishes," Francisco promised. "I would try to make friends with the Indians."

Mendoza nodded. "You are a real gentleman, I know," he said. "You would keep your promise and be fair with everyone." He sighed, then went on, "I, too, wish to see the New World, perhaps to make my fortune there. Like you, I am a second son, with no property in Spain. There is unknown land north of Mexico," the older man continued, "land still to be explored. . . . Perhaps we shall go to New Spain together."

4

New Spain

The group of armored horsemen stopped on a wooded hilltop. Below them was an island on a lake. On the island was a city. "Mexico City!" shouted the knights.

Twenty-five-year-old Francisco was one of the horsemen. He was helping escort Viceroy Mendoza to his new capital. Mendoza would rule New Spain for King Charles. New Spain was the name for today's Mexico, Central America, the Caribbean Islands, and northern Venezuela.

Coronado galloped with the other knights onto a stone road. It had been built above the water and led into the beautiful island city. A great parade of horsemen and men on foot met the knights at the city gate. Trumpeters in bright cloaks played tunes. Drummers pounded. Men cheered.

The newcomers were led through the wide, straight streets of the Spanish city. It was built on the ruins of Aztec palaces and temples destroyed by Cortés fourteen years before. The year was now 1535. Cortés himself was away, exploring New Spain's western coast by ship.

The parade ended at a great open square, the heart of Mexico City. Red stone government buildings, palaces, shops, and a church were built around the square. Mendoza's party was shown to seats before the Viceroy's palace.

The town crier read the King's orders. They ended, "Salute Antonio de Mendoza, First Viceroy of New Spain!" A mighty cheer arose. Church bells rang. Then knights of New Spain held a tournament in the square. A great feast in the palace ended the celebration.

That night, Francisco was given a room in the palace. He was to be Mendoza's secretary.

Francisco's work began at once. He must go everywhere with Mendoza. He must arrange meetings, take notes, and write letters.

First, Mendoza and Francisco inspected Mexico City. They saw the Indians building houses for the Spaniards. The Indians looked with hate at their Spanish rulers. Francisco remembered his mother's goodbye on his last visit home. "Treat the

Indians kindly," she had said, "as a Christian nobleman should."

Soon Mendoza took Francisco on trips to distant parts of Mexico. "I must see the other cities," Mendoza told Francisco, "and meet their officers."

Francisco enjoyed the trips, but he was always glad to return to Mexico City. He had met a beautiful girl there. She was Señorita Beatríz de Estrada. The poor people called her "Saint Beatríz," because she was so good to them.

Francisco himself was noble and kind. And he was one of the best-looking young men in New Spain. Within two years, dark-eyed Beatríz and Francisco were married.

Beatríz' father had been of royal blood. He was the treasurer of New Spain when he died. Her mother, Doña Estrada, was rich and charming. She gave the young couple a large ranch outside Mexico City. She also gave them her palace on the city square.

Before long, Francisco and Beatríz had a baby girl. They named her Isabel, for Francisco's mother. "I am the happiest man in New Spain," Francisco told his wife.

5

Golden Dreams

Francisco worked hard. He helped Mendoza plan new roads and better ways of farming and mining. Mendoza saw to it that the Indians were treated more fairly. Soon he was called "The Good Viceroy." Francisco was one of his chief assistants.

Francisco's army training was useful. There was a revolt in New Galicia, New Spain's northwest state. Coronado and his soldiers put down the revolt.

Mendoza was pleased with his secretary. He appointed Francisco to the Mexico City Council which governed the capital. It was a great honor for a young man.

Months later, Francisco was honored again. "Francisco," Mendoza said, "the Governor of New Galicia has died. You will be the new Governor."

Francisco was thrilled. Then he thought of Beatríz and Isabel. "What about my family?" he asked.

Mendoza smiled. "You cannot take them to the Northwest. It is too wild and dangerous. But you will come back to Mexico City often." Then Mendoza went on, "I have other plans, too. Do you remember the four shipwrecked men who came here two years ago?"

Francisco's eyes lighted. "How could I forget them?" he said. "They told of a land to the north that is rich with gold. I still wish we could explore it."

The two men fell silent, remembering what had happened two years before. Three ragged white men and one Negro had reported to Mendoza. Their leader was a nobleman named Cabeza de Vaca. They were part of the expedition of a Spaniard named Pánfilo de Narváez. Narváez and 400 men had explored the land north and west of Florida.

"Hostile Indians forced our expedition to the coast," Cabeza de Vaca had said. "We built five boats and sailed west, hoping to reach Mexico."

"What happened then?" Mendoza had asked.

"The boats leaked," Cabeza answered, "and sank in a storm. Most of the men drowned. Others of us who swam to shore were killed by hostile Indians. We four, the only survivors, lived as slaves of the Indians on an island and on the nearby coast for almost six years. Then we managed to escape, moving west from one tribe to another for two years. Finally, we walked south into New Galicia."

Estevan, the big Negro, held up a gourd rattle with feather streamers. "I found this medicine man's rattle," he grinned. "The Indians thought it was magic. When they saw it, they helped us on our way."

"We heard of a rich country to the north," Cabeza de Vaca added. "It has gold-trimmed houses. It may be richer than Mexico or Peru."

Mendoza had been interested at once. "We must ask King Charles's permission to explore it!" he had said.

Now Mendoza's dark eyes looked into

Francisco's blue ones. "King Charles has at last given permission for an expedition north," Mendoza said softly. "But we must pay for it ourselves."

Francisco listened eagerly.

"I have a plan," Mendoza went on. "I will send Estevan north to scout the golden country. Friar Marcos, the missionary, will go with him, for he gets on well with the Indians. If the land is really rich, I will send an expedition there."

Francisco's blue eyes shone with excitement. "I will help you plan the expedition," he promised.

A few months later, Francisco was in Culiacán. It was the most northern town in New Galicia. He was saying good-bye to Estevan and Friar Marcos. Friar Onorato was leaving too. They were going to scout the northern land.

"I will save many Indian souls," Friar Marcos said quietly.

"I will find gold," the jolly Negro laughed. He danced about, shaking his gourd rattle with the bright feathers. Tiny bells jingled on Estevan's wrists and ankles. "The Indians will do anything for me when they see my rattle," he boasted.

"Go with God," Governor Coronado said, watching Estevan and the two friars start north. Indian guides and supply bearers went with them. Friar Onorato soon became ill and turned back.

Three months later, Friar Marcos returned alone to Culiacán. He hurried to Compostela to see Coronado. "Estevan went ahead with the Indian guides," the friar told Coronado. "He sent runners back to me with crosses. A cross as big as a man's hand meant good land. The richer the land, the bigger the cross is."

"Did he send big crosses?" Coronado asked eagerly.

"As tall as a man," the friar nodded. "The scouts told of seven rich cities ahead, in a country called Cíbola. They heard that Cíbola's houses have golden doors trimmed with turquoise."

Friar Marcos went on, "An old story tells of seven Portuguese bishops escaping from the Moors. They sailed west and built seven golden cities across the Ocean Sea. The seven cities of Cíbola must have been built by the bishops."

"But where is Estevan?" Coronado asked.

"Dead," was the sad reply. "His rattle meant nothing to the Cíbolans. I met three of his guides on the road, and they told me that Estevan and all the other guides had been killed."

"What?" cried Coronado in dismay. "Then you yourself never saw Cíbola?"

"Oh, yes," the friar answered. "I climbed a hill and saw the first city from afar. It shone like gold in the sun. It is larger than Mexico City. I set up a cross and claimed the land for Spain."

The big friar sighed. "Then I turned back with much more fear than food, and traveled with all the speed I could make. . . ."

"We must go to Mexico City at once," Coronado cried, "and report to Viceroy Mendoza. I will ask him to send an expedition north."

6

Parade of Gentlemen

When he reached Mexico City, Coronado hurried to see his family. By now, there was a second little daughter, Marina. How he had missed them all!

Next, Coronado and Friar Marcos reported to Mendoza. They told him about the land of gold. "I will send an expedition north," Mendoza decided. "Francisco, you must help plan it. Choose the men and buy the supplies."

Mexico City was full of Spanish knights. Most were younger sons seeking their fortunes. All were eager to join the expedition.

Cortés himself came to Coronado. He had finished exploring the west coast, and was living in his mountain palace near Mexico City. "Please ask Mendoza to let me lead the expedition," Cortés said.

Coronado remembered his boyhood admiration for Cortés. He looked at the bent, graying man, now lame in an arm and a leg. "I will ask Mendoza," he promised. And he did.

But Mendoza smiled, "You, Francisco, will be General of the expedition."

Coronado's heart leaped. He could hardly wait to tell Beatríz. "I am proud," she said. "But we will miss you so much. God grant your safe return."

On February 22, 1540, the great expedition gathered on the plain beside Compostela, capital of New Galicia. General Coronado wore gilded armor. White plumes waved from his shining helmet. He sat on his horse beside Viceroy Mendoza. The Viceroy would return to Mexico City as soon as the expedition was well under way.

Facing them were 225 armored knights on prancing horses. More than 60 foot soldiers in buckskin carried spears, crossbows, or muskets. Several hundred Indians brought up the rear. They were scouts, supply bearers, and cattle and sheep herders. A thousand sheep and cattle, to be used for fresh meat, were going with the explorers.

Other supplies would follow the expedition by ship. Friar Marcos had said the trail north was never far from the Gulf of California.

A trumpet blew to call the men to attention. Viceroy Mendoza spoke. "Claim new land for Spain," he ordered. "Make friends with the Indians. Teach them the Christian faith. Never fight them, unless they attack you. Obey your General always."

The men gave a mighty cheer. "Coronado! Coronado!"

Thirty-year-old Coronado placed his hand on a Bible. It was the proudest moment of his life. "I promise to obey my God and my King," he said in a loud, clear voice. "I shall lead my men fearlessly. I shall take the Christian faith to the Indians."

The explorers began to file past Coronado. The captains came first. Among them were stern Cárdenas, laughing

Alvarado, and Maldonado, a champion horseman. Each gave his name, swearing to obey the General. A doctor followed the captains. The sun was low before all the men had passed.

The next day, the expedition started north. Coronado, with his gilded armor and plumed helmet, looked like a king on horseback. Flag-bearers waved red and

yellow banners. Trumpets and drums
sounded. Knights and footmen laughed
and sang. Horses whinnied. Mooing cattle
and bleating sheep straggled along behind.

Mendoza rode with the expedition for a
while, then turned back to Mexico City.
"It is a parade of gentlemen led by a
gentleman," he said as he waved good-bye.

Coronado was sad to see his friend

leave. He knew Mendoza longed to lead the expedition himself. But it might take years to find gold.

Suddenly Coronado's face clouded. What if there were no gold ahead? He thought of the money Mendoza had put into the expedition. He remembered all that Beatríz had spent for supplies. And many young knights had given everything they had, hoping to find treasure and become rich.

But who could be gloomy on such an exciting day? Coronado smiled. "We cannot fail," he decided.

7

The Long Trail

The expedition headed for Culiacán. Friar Marcos and three other friars had gone on ahead. The trail led through swampy land near the sea. The horses skidded over the slippery paths. They shied at snakes and alligators.

Culiacán was 300 miles away. The army did not reach it for a month.

There Coronado called his men together. "There are so many of us that we move very slowly. We must divide into two groups. I will lead a small, fast party north. The others will follow us in twenty days."

Coronado chose 70 horsemen, 300 foot soldiers, and the best Indian helpers. The friars would go with him, too.

The trail from Culiacán led up steep mountains. Scouts spread out, seeking fresh food from Indian villages. But the Indians' crops were poor. They had barely enough food for themselves.

The soldiers grew hungry and cross. The horses grew weak from lack of food.

"Save the horses' strength!" Coronado ordered. He cheerfully got off his own horse and walked. His horse now only carried his baggage.

The young knights followed Coronado's example. "The General has 23 horses with him," one knight said to another. "Yet he walks, as we do."

"Where is the land of gold?" the soldiers asked.

"The seven cities of Cíbola are not far," Friar Marcos comforted them. "And the supply ships with food are only fifteen miles away."

Coronado asked some friendly Indians the way to the sea and the supply ships. "The coast is fifteen days away," the Indians said.

That meant fifteen days of marching each way! Not the Friar's fifteen miles! Coronado could not wait there for a month. The ships would have to explore the coast alone.

Coronado ordered his men to move on

north. "We will have to do without the extra supplies," he said. "The food we have must be made to last as long as possible."

Finally, the explorers reached today's Arizona. It was desert land. The men and horses burned with thirst. Many horses died of starvation. One Spaniard died, too, after eating the poisonous loco-weed. Coronado remembered Narváez' 400 men. All but a very few had died at sea. Would his men die in a desert?

The desert ended at the White Mountains. Here the trail led through a rocky wilderness. The daily food rations became smaller and smaller. The horses were too weak to carry men or packs. The men, faint with hunger, staggered up the steep mountains.

At last the explorers reached a swift

river, the Zuñi. It was now July, eleven weeks since the expedition had left Culiacán. Suddenly, four strange Indians appeared beside the river. Their hands were raised in the sign of peace. "They are Cíbolans," one of Coronado's Indian helpers said. "Do not trust them. Remember that they killed Estevan."

The Spaniards, too, gave the sign of peace. The Indians disappeared. The expedition moved on.

That night, the army camped near a mountain pass that led into Cíbola. Coronado ordered sentries to guard the pass. Soon after midnight, the noise of fighting woke the men. "The Cíbolans are attacking!" cried the guards.

At once, Coronado's knights made ready for battle. Some of the young knights were so excited that they put saddles on

their horses backwards. They all dashed into the mountain pass, shouting, "Santiago!" It was the old Spanish battle cry.

The Indians faded away into the darkness.

The Spaniards returned to camp. Soon fires could be seen on the mountaintops. "Those are signal fires," Coronado's Indian guides told him. "They are ordering all Cíbolans to rise against the strangers."

8

Battle of Cíbola

In the morning the army started out again. Coronado sent scouts ahead to look for Indians. "We must try to make friends with the Cíbolans," Coronado told his men. But no Cíbolans were seen.

The explorers wound around steep, flat-topped mountains which they called *mesas*, from the Spanish word for "table."

As the Spaniards rounded the last mesa, they saw a plain ahead. Across the plain was a strange Indian village. It was near today's Zuñi, New Mexico. "Cíbola!" cried Friar Marcos.

The men stopped, staring in dismay. "The walls are not gold!" shouted a soldier angrily. "They're nothing but rocks and dried mud."

Coronado, too, was dismayed at the poorness of the village, or pueblo. It was like a four-story apartment house, built around a square. The first floor had a small gateway in its solid wall. The upper floors were set back like giant steps. The edges of the roofs were lined with big stones. No Indians were in sight.

"Friar Marcos!" Coronado began angrily.

But the friar had disappeared to the rear. Gray-robed Friar Juan de Padilla was in his place. "There may be no gold," the tall friar said softly. "But there are Indians to be converted."

Suddenly, hundreds of Indians rushed through the pueblo gate. They carried leather shields, bows and arrows, and war clubs. They drew up on the plain opposite the Spaniards.

A chief in war paint sprinkled a line of corn on the ground between the Indians and the Spaniards. "He says you must not cross that line," an Indian guide told Coronado.

Coronado spoke to Captain Cárdenas. The captain, Friar Padilla, Friar Luis, and an army clerk moved up to the line. The clerk read a letter to the Indians from King Charles. It ended, "You now belong to Spain and the Catholic Church."

When the words were translated, the

Cíbolans laughed. An arrow pinned Friar Luis' robe to the ground.

Now Coronado and a few horsemen rode up to the chief, carrying gifts. The Indians jeered more loudly. They shot arrows at the horses' feet. The horses reared. The Cíbolans screamed with glee. "They call you cowards!" a guide told Coronado.

Coronado turned to Friar Padilla. "Do we retreat as cowards?" he asked, "or do we fight as Spaniards?"

The good friar, once a soldier, answered sadly, "We must fight, or leave this land forever."

Coronado raised his sword, shouting, "Santiago!"

Every Spaniard echoed the battle cry. Foot soldiers weak from hunger shot their heavy crossbows and muskets. Horsemen dashed into the crowd of Cíbolans. The warriors fell back to their pueblo. Some crowded through the gate. Others climbed ladders, let down from above. Then they pulled up the ladders.

The Spaniards galloped after the Indians and up to the pueblo wall. The Indians threw rocks down from their roofs.

Suddenly, Coronado saw a forgotten ladder against the pueblo wall. He leaped

from his horse and ran toward the ladder. His captains followed.

The Cíbolans hurled rocks and arrows at Coronado. His shining helmet was dented, but not pierced. A great stone knocked him down. He got up and ran on.

Suddenly, a larger rock landed squarely on his helmet. Coronado fell, unconscious. Captains Cárdenas and Alvarado crouched over him, protecting him from more blows.

Then other men carried the fallen general behind the lines.

Nothing could stop the angry Spaniards now. They drove the Cíbolans from the pueblo in an hour. Their shouts of victory awoke Coronado.

The General got up shakily. He followed his men into the pueblo. Great storerooms were filled with food—dried deer meat, corn, and beans. Already the men were cooking the food over open fires.

"This is better than gold," Coronado heard a hungry soldier say. "We could not eat gold."

Coronado feasted with the rest, but he felt ill and worried. The first city of Cíbola held no gold. The Indians were hostile. And Friar Marcos' tales of treasure were not true. Was there any gold at all in this northern land?

9

Land of the Pueblos

Coronado set up his headquarters in the pueblo. He sent out scouts in every direction. They found five other pueblos in Cíbola, not six. They found only a few turquoises, and no gold.

Stern Captain Cárdenas led some scouts west. Returning, they told Coronado excitedly, "We saw the deepest canyon in the world. We could not climb down the side of the canyon to the river below." They had discovered the Grand Canyon of the Colorado River, but they had found no gold.

Coronado sent messengers back to Mexico City with letters for Mendoza and Beatríz. He sent Friar Marcos with them, ordering him not to return. "He has not told the truth about anything," Coronado wrote Mendoza.

What golden city had the friar seen? A mirage or shimmering picture in the desert air? A cloud castle? Tower-like mountain peaks gleaming in the sun? No one will ever know.

In late August some friendly Indians came to Coronado. Their leader was a young chief with a mustache. The Spaniards called him "Whiskers."

"We come from the Pecos River, to the east," he said. "We live near great plains. We will take you to see the big humpbacked beasts on the plains. Here are some of their skins." The Indians unrolled some shaggy buffalo skins.

"Alvarado!" Coronado called to his gay young captain. "Marco Polo wrote of humpbacked beasts in Asia. This New Land may be part of Asia, after all." He gave Alvarado his orders. "Take twenty men east with Whiskers, to see the strange animals."

Soon it was fall. Coronado's Indian helpers warned of the long, hard winter in Cíbola. "We must have shelter from the blizzards and the cold," they said. "There will be huge snowdrifts. It will be impossible to travel during the winter."

Coronado expected the main army to

arrive soon. The Cíbolan pueblo was too small to hold them all. What should they do?

Just then, a messenger arrived from Alvarado. "We saw the humpbacked cows, but no gold," Alvarado's report said. "There is a land between Cíbola and the Pecos River, called Tiguex. It has 80 pueblos. It could shelter our whole expedition. We will wait for you there."

Coronado smiled for the first time in many days. "We shall go to Tiguex," he decided, "as soon as the rest of the army arrives."

The first snows were falling when the main army appeared. Together they all plodded east, through forests and over black lava rocks. At last they reached the first pueblo of Tiguex.

Alvarado's men welcomed them with

shouts of joy. "The Indians have left us this pueblo and all their food and blankets," Alvarado told Coronado proudly. "It is big enough for us all."

The walls of the pueblo were made of sun-dried brick. They were built better than those of Cíbola. The pueblo was on the Rio Grande River, near what is today Bernalillo, New Mexico.

Alvarado brought a tall Indian wearing a turban to Coronado. "We call him the Turk," Alvarado laughed, "because of his headpiece. The Pecos River Indians captured him in a war. Hear his story."

The Turk bowed low and spoke with sign language. "I am from Harahey, near Quivira, far northeast of here," he began. "Quivira is a land of gold, with golden houses. It has a great river with fish as big as horses. My chief rides in a gold-

trimmed canoe paddled by 40 men. He eats from gold plates. He sleeps under a tree full of golden bells making sweet music. When the snow melts, I will lead you there."

"Do you have any gold with you?" Coronado asked.

"I had a gold bracelet," the Turk answered. "But Whiskers took it from me."

Whiskers had returned to his people, the Pecos River Indians. Coronado sent Alvarado and a few men after him. They asked Whiskers for the bracelet. Whiskers angrily replied, "It is a lie! Your Turk never had a gold bracelet."

Alvarado took Whiskers to Coronado. Whiskers stayed in Tiguex as a prisoner all winter. He stuck to his story that the Turk was a liar.

The days grew colder and colder. Bands

of soldiers went to other Tiguex pueblos, seeking more blankets. Cárdenas cruelly attacked one pueblo and killed most of its people. Coronado was angry at Cárdenas, but he could not undo the damage. The people of Tiguex rebelled against the Spanish and fought them bitterly for months. Deep snows finally ended the fighting.

10

Humpbacked Cows

At last the snows melted. In April, 1541, Coronado's entire army set out for Quivira, land of gold. Once more the men laughed and sang. The Turk led them. Sopete, another captive from Quivira, went along, too.

Each day a soldier "counter" counted his long, even steps. Tramp, tramp, tramp. "One, two, three . . . ninety-seven, ninety-eight, ninety-nine," he droned. From the number of steps, they could figure out how many miles they had marched.

The Spaniards marched over the mountains to Whiskers' big pueblo, located on the Pecos River. His people greeted him joyfully.

"We will give you corn for your journey," Whiskers told Coronado.

Just then, the Turk appeared. "Don't load your horses with food," he said to Coronado. "There is plenty of food everywhere."

Sopete turned on the Turk angrily. "Liar!" the Indian boy cried out.

The General wisely took the corn.

The army followed the Turk south and east to the place known today as the Great Plains. Coronado looked with wonder across the endless prairie. "It is like being inside a bowl," he wrote later.

"Wherever a man stands, the sky hems him in."

Soon the explorers saw milling herds of brown animals. "The humpbacked cows!" they cried. A few young knights set out to hunt them.

The buffaloes turned upon the horsemen and charged with lowered horns. The hunters escaped with their lives, but some horses were killed.

The expedition marched on, over the plains of tall grass. The grass was so wiry that it sprang up again as soon as the men moved on. One of the explorers wrote, ". . . a thousand horses and 500 cows and more than 5,000 rams and ewes and more than 1,500 friendly Indian servants traveling over these plains would leave no more trace than if nothing had been there."

The Spaniards saw only a few Indians. They were wandering tribes who lived on buffalo meat. They moved their buffalo-hide tepees on sleds. Dogs pulled the sleds over the smooth grass.

More than a month passed. The hungry soldiers killed buffaloes for food. The only water came from muddy buffalo ponds. It made the men sick. Where was Quivira?

At last the expedition found a great canyon along a clear stream. Low cedar trees gave some welcome shade. It was Tule Canyon, in today's Texas Panhandle. "We shall rest here a few days," Coronado decided.

Suddenly, a terrible storm arose. A black cloud roared into the canyon. Hailstones fell, as big as duck eggs. The hail dented the Spaniards' armor and tore

their tents. It broke every dish and cut the horses.

The men ran into caves in the canyon walls. The horses followed them or hid beneath the low trees.

After the storm, Coronado called his captains together. "Shall we still follow the Turk?" he asked.

"Bring in Sopete," one captain said. "Ask him where Quivira is. He says the Turk leads us astray."

Sopete came into the torn tent. He threw himself at Coronado's feet. "The Turk lies!" he cried. "Quivira is my land. It is not as rich as he says. It is north of here, yet he leads you southeast. Let me lead you to Quivira!"

The captains voted to follow Sopete.

The army turned north. When they reached Palo Duro (Hardwood) Canyon,

Coronado told his men, "We are marching too slowly to reach Quivira before fall. The winter snows will catch us without shelter. I must lead a few fast horsemen north, as I did into Cíbola. The main army, with the herds, will return to Tiguex for another winter."

11

Quivira

Every explorer wanted to go north with Coronado. The General chose 30 horsemen, 6 foot soldiers, 40 Indian workers, and brave Friar Padilla. The Turk would follow them in chains.

The small force set out at once. It was led by Sopete and a compass-bearer. The bearer hung his compass from a silk thread. It was a small magnet, like a needle. It always pointed north.

The explorers marched from Texas through today's Oklahoma Panhandle. Then they went into Kansas. They came to the great Arkansas River. Here they met a hunting party from Quivira. The Indians were dressed in dirty skins.

Coronado turned angrily to the Turk. "Are these the richly dressed, jeweled people of Quivira?" he thundered.

The Turk could lie no longer. He answered rudely, "Yes, I fooled you. I promised the people of Tiguex to lose you on the buffalo plains. We hoped you would starve there." Then he added slyly, "But I can still show you treasure north of Quivira."

So the Spaniards kept the chained Turk with them.

Now the party headed northeast. They finally reached the first village of Quivira. It was near what is today the city of Lyons, Kansas.

Coronado and his men frowned in disappointment at the Indians' huts. They were round with pointed tops, like giant beehives. Golden thatch covered each hut from tip to ground. These were the Turk's "golden houses."

Big, friendly Indians ran to greet the strangers. Tall Chief Tatarrax strode up to General Coronado. The chief wore a great feather headdress. A strange copper ornament hung from a string around his neck.

Coronado and Chief Tatarrax talked politely in sign language. Coronado pointed to the copper ornament. "Where did it come from?" he asked.

"From far away." The chief pointed north. He gave the ornament to Coronado.

The General bowed his thanks. He thought sadly, "This is the only metal we have found in the New Land."

The Indians spread a feast on the ground for their guests. There were corn, melons, grapes, nuts, beans, and berries. The Spaniards ate hungrily.

Coronado stayed in Quivira almost a month, exploring today's central Kansas. "This is wonderful farmland," he told his captains.

"It's too far from New Spain to settle," answered one.

"There's no gold," grumbled another.

Only Friar Padilla and Sopete were happy. The friar put up a tall, wooden cross, higher than a man. He taught the Indians to fold their hands, praying to the Christian God. Sopete returned to his own home, to stay.

But the Turk tried to turn the Indians of Quivira against the Spaniards. "Kill the strangers!" he demanded. "Kill them and set me free!"

Hearing of this, Coronado's captains said angrily, "The Turk must die as a traitor!"

Coronado agreed sadly. That night, the Turk was put to death.

It was now August, 1541. "We must return to Tiguex before snowfall," Coronado decided. "In the spring, the entire army will explore farther north."

Guides from Quivira led Coronado's men back to Tiguex. Each morning a guide sighted the rising sun. Then he faced about and shot an arrow southwest. The explorers marched to the arrow. Then another arrow was shot, in the same direction. Marching in a straight line, the Spaniards reached Tiguex in six weeks.

"It was only 520 miles from Quivira to Tiguex," Coronado told his captains. "But we marched 850 miles, going to Quivira. The Turk led us 330 miles astray."

12

Fall from a Horse

Christmas Day, 1541, came and went at the Spaniards' winter quarters in Tiguex. "The men are bored," Coronado told his captains, "and so am I." He turned to dark-haired Captain Maldonado, their best horseman. "You and I must have a horse race, Maldonado," he said.

Everyone rushed from the pueblo onto
the plain. "Saddle my fastest horse,
Pedro," Coronado called to his Indian
servant. "Put on the new girth I have
never used before."

Grinning, the boy obeyed. He did not
notice that the leather girth was dry and
cracked. He buckled it around the horse's
middle, to hold the saddle in place.

Coronado and Maldonado rode to a track which the soldiers had cleared in the snow. The horses were off, neck and neck. The cheering soldiers shouted, "Coronado! Maldonado!"

Suddenly Coronado's girth broke. His saddle slipped off. The General was thrown under Maldonado's horse. A flying hoof hit Coronado's head. He lay like one dead.

Soldiers carried their general gently to his quarters. The expedition's one doctor examined Coronado's wound. "I am afraid his brain is injured," the doctor said. "I cannot tell if he will live or die."

Days passed before Coronado spoke. Then he thought he was home, and called for Beatríz. All winter he lay on his cot. He seemed to come and go between the real world and a dream world. He remembered Iago's farewell, years ago in Salamanca. "You will win much power in a distant land. But beware of a bad fall which you may never get over."

Coronado had won power in a distant land. He had fallen in the battle of Cíbola but had recovered. Would he ever get over this fall?

When his mind was clear, Coronado thought back over his explorations. He had now been in the New Land over two years. He had found no gold. He had one copper ornament from the north, but the copper mines were too far away to pay for the mining. Was there any use in exploring farther?

"I have claimed more land for Spain than anyone expected," Coronado thought. "And the friars have converted many Indians. I have won every battle with the Indians and have lost very few men. We should return home to New Spain while we can."

One of the soldiers brought Coronado a paper asking to go home. Most of the men had signed it.

Coronado called his captains to his bedside. "Shall we explore north of Quivira this spring?" he asked. "Or shall we go home?"

The captains voted to go home as soon as the snow melted.

By spring, however, a few men had changed their minds. "We wish to go north by ourselves," they told Coronado.

But the General answered, "The Indians would wipe out a small group. They do not dare attack our whole army. You promised to obey me in Compostela. I order everyone south."

These men began to grumble behind Coronado's back. "We could find gold in the north," one said.

"The General is just homesick," another added. "He wants to see his family."

Only the friars thought the expedition a real success. "We have converted many Indians," brave Friar Padilla told Coronado. "I am going back to Quivira to convert the whole country. The other friars will stay to help the Indians in the pueblo country."

The General could not order missionaries to leave their work. Years later, three of Friar Padilla's helpers returned to New Spain. They told of the friar's death. He had been shot by the arrows of Quivira's enemies.

13

Homecoming

In April, 1542, Coronado's army began the sad march home. The best planned expedition of the Americas was returning, empty-handed.

The General had not yet recovered fully from his accident. He was too weak to ride a horse, so his Indian servants made a hammock for him. It swung between two mules, walking one behind the other.

Coronado, one of the King's best horse-men, felt disgraced.

The long, ragged parade wound through the desert of New Mexico. The desert was bright with spring flowers, but Coronado did not see them. He closed his eyes against the blinding sun. His head ached all the time.

The army struggled through the mountains of Arizona and south into New Spain. At Culiacán, Coronado dismissed many of his men. The Indians went to their forest homes. The Spaniards found work on farms or in business.

More men dropped out in Compostela where the expedition had started. There the General bought a gentle horse. He hoped to be able to ride soon.

It was fall before Coronado neared Mexico City. He had been gone almost three years. He mounted his new horse outside the city. Less than 100 men were still with their leader. "Enter the city a few at a time," he told them. "People might laugh at us if we paraded, for we have no gold."

Coronado rode straight to his palace on the great square. "Will Beatríz be angry with me?" he worried. "I lost all the money she gave for the expedition. Will Viceroy Mendoza punish me for losing his money, too?"

The great door of his house opened. All at once, Coronado's loving family was around him. Beatríz and the little girls cried for joy. "But you are so thin!" Beatríz wailed. "You must go to bed. We will nurse you back to health."

Sinking into his soft bed, Coronado was almost happy.

In a few days, Viceroy Mendoza visited his sick General. "I found no gold," Coronado said sadly, "but I lost less than 30 Indians. I paid my Indian helpers fair wages. They are my friends. And many Indians in the New Land are now Christians."

"You could not find gold if there was none," Mendoza answered slowly. "You claimed a vast country for Spain. Yours is the only expedition to have won every battle."

Coronado smiled with relief. He felt even better when Mendoza went on, "You are still on the Mexico City Council, and still Governor of New Galicia." In a month, Coronado was attending Council meetings.

After awhile Coronado moved his family to Guadalajara. This was the new capital

of New Galicia. He took up his work as governor there.

A king's judge came to New Galicia to question Coronado. Some of the explorers had written to the king. They blamed the General for not exploring farther. "Why did you come home so soon?" the judge asked.

Coronado tried to explain. Sometimes he had to hold his aching head and reply, "I forget."

Finally the judge wrote the king, "Coronado is not the same man he was. . . . They say this change was caused by the fall from a horse." The judge thought that Coronado was too ill to be governor. Coronado agreed.

The Coronado family moved back to Mexico City. The work of the council took only part of Coronado's time. He could spend many days on his nearby sheep ranch.

In a few years, the king gave Coronado more ranchland. "It is in honor of my exploration," he told Beatríz proudly. "We can now raise more fine sheep."

Isabel and Marina were growing up. When Isabel became engaged, Coronado was too ill to work. He was only 44, but his health was broken. "Your future husband can attend council meetings in my place," he told Isabel.

Soon afterward, in September, 1554, Coronado died. He was buried under the altar in Santo Domingo Church, three blocks from the Mexico City square. There he and his family lie, to this day.

No more great expeditions explored the New World after Coronado did. Instead, Spanish settlers gradually moved onto the land he had discovered. In time, the land became a part of the United States of America.

Today, farms and ranches cover Quivira and Coronado's buffalo plains. Silver, gold, and copper are among the minerals found in his mountains. "Black gold," the oil of Oklahoma and Texas, lay under the explorers' feet. Uranium, the most precious mineral of all, is now mined in the pueblo country. These are the riches of the great American Southwest, discovered by the noble General Francisco Vásquez de Coronado.